CLASS IN AMERICA

CLASS AND RACE

BY DUCHESS HARRIS, JD, PHD

WITH LAURA K. MURRAY

Essential Library

An Imprint of Abdo Publishing | abdopublishing.com

ABDOPUBLISHING.COM

Published by Abdo Publishing, a division of ABDO, PO Box 398166, Minneapolis, Minnesota 55439.
Copyright © 2019 by Abdo Consulting Group, Inc. International copyrights reserved in all countries.
No part of this book may be reproduced in any form without written permission from the publisher.
Essential Library™ is a trademark and logo of Abdo Publishing.

Printed in the United States of America, North Mankato, Minnesota
032018
092018

THIS BOOK CONTAINS RECYCLED MATERIALS

Cover Photo: Antonova Katya/Shutterstock Images
Interior Photos: Jake May/The Flint Journal-MLive.com/AP Images, 5; Paul Sancya/AP Images, 9; Carlos Osorio/AP Images, 11; Ryan DeBerardinis/Shutterstock Images, 13; MPI/Archive Photos/Getty Images, 17; Library of Congress/Corbis/Getty Images, 21; Vladimir Korostyshevskiy/Shutterstock Images, 22–23; Everett Historical/Shutterstock Images, 27, 31; AP Images, 34, 54, 68; Shutterstock Images, 37, 61, 83; Monkey Business Images/Shutterstock Images, 40, 70; Bettmann/Getty Images, 45; Bebeto Matthews/AP Images, 49; Photo12/Universal Images Group/Getty Images, 52–53; Jason Redmond/AP Images, 58; Nick Tropiano/Shutterstock Images, 65; Sid Hastings/AP Images, 73; Sarah A. Miller/Tyler Morning Telegraph/AP Images, 78; Charles Krupa/AP Images, 80; Jim Watson/AFP/Getty Images, 87; Jae C. Hong/AP Images, 90; Joel Martinez/The Monitor/AP Images, 93; Steve Helber/AP Images, 97; Alex Milan Tracy/Sipa USA/AP Images, 98

Editor: Arnold Ringstad
Series Designer: Becky Daum

LIBRARY OF CONGRESS CONTROL NUMBER: 2017961139

PUBLISHER'S CATALOGING-IN-PUBLICATION DATA

Names: Harris, Duchess, author. | Murray, Laura K., author.
Title: Class and race / by Duchess Harris and Laura K. Murray.
Description: Minneapolis, Minnesota : Abdo Publishing, 2019. | Series: Class in America | Includes
        online resources and index.
Identifiers: ISBN 9781532114069 (lib.bdg.) | ISBN 9781532153891 (ebook)
Subjects: LCSH: Race relations--Juvenile literature. | Social classes--Juvenile literature. | Equality
        --United States--Juvenile literature. | Occupations and race--Juvenile literature. | Social
        classes--United States--History--Juvenile literature.
Classification: DDC 301.451--dc23

CONTENTS

ONE

FIGHTING
FOR FLINT

T he water in Flint, Michigan, the city in which
eight-year-old Amariyanna "Mari" Copeny lived, was not
safe to drink. It smelled terrible. It caused headaches,
rashes, and illnesses. Seeing many other children who lived in
Flint getting sick and suffering, Copeny decided something
needed to be done. She began speaking out about the water
crisis. She traveled to Washington, DC, to attend congressional
hearings. She went to rallies and spoke with news media. She
helped organize the distribution of bottled water and raised
money for a nonprofit that provides school supplies to Flint
children. In May 2016, Copeny wrote to President Barack Obama:
"I've been doing my best to march in protest and to speak out

Mari Copeny spoke out about the Flint, Michigan,
water crisis in 2016.

ENVIRONMENTAL INJUSTICE

As was the case with Flint, minority and poor communities face the worst effects of environmental hazards and pollution. This is sometimes referred to as environmental injustice or racism. Segregated neighborhoods have been found to have more toxic waste sites and landfills than wealthier communities or areas with fewer minority residents. These environmental factors can be harmful to people's health. Some researchers suggest that these communities do not have the same type of political power as other areas to prevent undesirable construction or development. In addition, it may be more difficult for residents to move away.

The issue of environmental justice came to the forefront with Hurricane Katrina's destruction of the Gulf South in 2005. A 2008 report found that the racial disparities of the damage came from many years of environmental injustice. Report author Reilly Morse remarked on the lack of damage in affluent areas compared with poor and minority areas. Morse wrote that, unlike poorer areas, affluent neighborhoods had "high elevations and low exposure to riverside nuisances such as industrial sites, railroads, and wharves, or back-swamp nuisances such as floods, mosquitoes, unpaved roads, and dumps. They also had convenient access to public transportation and adequate urban infrastructure. Finally, these neighborhoods generally did not find themselves forced to accept intrusive developments, such as overhead highways or industrial canals."[2] The report also criticized the government's evacuation and disaster response for not properly assisting low-income or minority neighborhoods.

for all the kids that live here in Flint."[1] A few months later, Obama visited Flint to see the crisis firsthand.

The problems in Flint had begun about two years earlier, in April 2014, when the city's water source was switched from the Detroit, Michigan, water system to the Flint River. The move was meant to be temporary. To save money, the city planned to hook up to a new, cheaper water system that was yet to be completed. But because officials neglected to treat the corrosive river water properly, the water was leaching lead from the city's old pipes. Lead can cause serious, irreversible damage, especially to children's physical and mental development. Flint residents were being slowly poisoned.

The complaints of citizens, health officials, and activists were disregarded by state officials. Some people took matters into their own hands. They called in experts to help perform water quality testing. After damaging reports emerged, the city instructed some residents to boil their water before using it. Still, the city's officials continued to insist that Flint's water was safe for most of the population. Finally, in October 2015, Flint was reconnected to the Detroit water system. But the water problems were far from over. In January 2016, a federal state of emergency was declared, as unsafe lead levels remained in many homes. The National Guard arrived in Flint to distribute filters and bottles of water.

The damaging effects of the water crisis linger today for Flint residents. The city's water quality has improved to acceptable levels, but most residents continue to rely on bottled or filtered water at home.

LONG-TERM STRUGGLE

Local pediatrician Dr. Mona Hanna-Attisha helped expose the Flint crisis when she noticed a spike in the lead levels present in the bodies of the city's children. She noted that lead poisoning can have long-term effects on the future of communities. "If you were going to put something in a population to keep them down for generations to come, it would be lead," she remarked.[3]

DANGEROUS
WATER

In 2014, the water gushing from the faucets in LeeAnne Walters's Flint home was brown. Sometimes the foul-smelling water turned a bright yellow or a greasy red. Walters and her family were losing hair and eyelashes. Her children had developed rashes on their skin after bathing. One of them suffered from stomach pain, and another had stopped growing.

Something was wrong, and Walters knew the water was to blame. Testing showed her home's tap water had lead concentrations exceeding levels typically seen in hazardous waste. One of Walters's children tested positive for lead. Still, the city said the problem was limited to her home.

The mother of four teamed with Virginia Tech professor Marc Edwards, who provided hundreds of water testing kits to Flint residents. The tests showed that spiking lead levels were concentrated in the poorest areas of Flint. These areas also aligned with places in which children were found to have elevated lead levels in their blood. Walters is credited as a whistle-blower who spurred state officials to finally address Flint's water crisis. She continued her involvement in the aftermath of the crisis, testifying at a Senate hearing and in district court.

Flint residents were forced to rely on water from bottles or jugs while the city's water supply was fixed.

In March 2017, the Environmental Protection Agency (EPA) announced that it would provide $100 million to the city for upgrades to infrastructure. The city's vow to replace its 18,000 lead pipes was expected to take until at least 2020.[4] Meanwhile, experts warn that health problems caused by toxic water may appear years later. The State of Michigan, Governor Rick Snyder, the EPA, companies, and state officials face lawsuits. Several officials face criminal charges.

In the years since the crisis began, citizens like Copeny have continued their activism, urging the world to remember Flint. Many people have wondered how a water crisis could have happened in the United States. Others were not surprised.

CAUSES OF A CRISIS

More than 40 percent of Flint's residents lived in poverty, making it one of the poorest cities in the United States.[5] The city's economy had been in decline since large cuts to local automobile factories in the 1980s. Once home to General Motors factories, Flint was a working-class city built around the booming vehicle industry. Throughout the 1960s and 1970s, General Motors employed more than 80,000 people in Flint.[6] In the 1980s, a recession, high gas prices, and other factors hit the auto industry hard. General Motors closed Flint factories and laid off workers while opening plants in other countries. Wages and jobs continued to disappear from Flint in the following decades.

As the story of the water crisis made headlines, many experts insisted that such serious water problems would have been addressed much sooner in wealthier communities. Details emerged of officials who responded inadequately and downplayed the risks of the tainted water. Some critics charged that the incident showed racism and a lack of compassion for

Many Flint residents now live near massive empty lots that were once auto manufacturing plants.

people of color. At the time of the water crisis, approximately 56 percent of Flint's 100,000 residents were African American.[7]

In 2017, the Michigan Civil Rights Commission released a report. The report cited several factors going back decades that had led to the water crisis, including systemic racism and poverty. The report was clear about the issue of racism: "'Was race a factor in the Flint Water Crisis?' Our answer is an unreserved and undeniable—'yes.'"[8]

THE MAKING OF RACE

In the United States, many people think of race as being linked to someone's skin color or facial features, although other factors such as ancestry or religion may be used to identify race. But race does not have much to do with genetics or any science. Rather than biology, race is shaped by society and history. According to writer Brendon O'Flaherty, race has "something to do with culture and social networks, something to do with conventions, and even something to do with individual choice."[9] Ethnicity is different and usually has more to do with language, geography, and culture.

DEFINING RACE AND CLASS

The crisis and aftermath in Flint highlighted the issues of class and race in the United States. The entanglement of the two topics comes up in discussions of housing, education, employment, health care, and more. Race and class in the United States are deeply connected. They are both ways in which people think of themselves and ways in which society views—and treats— them. Race is a cultural concept, rather than a scientific one.

The United States is filled with a diverse population that experiences important intersections between class and race.

In the United States, race is often related to a person's skin color and ethnicity. African American, white, Asian, Hispanic, Pacific Islander, and many others are examples of racial identifiers. Class is related to a person's status in society. It is often thought of as a combination of factors, including income, wealth, housing, and education.

Some people have argued that the United States should embrace "color blindness." They say that events such as the 2008 election of Barack Obama as the country's first African American president point to a "post-racial America," meaning that people no longer discriminate or judge based on race.

STUCK ON THE LADDER

A mainstay of the American dream is social mobility—the ability to climb the rungs of the social ladder. Some argue that this idea is a myth because American citizens are not equal when it comes to social mobility. Different races experience discrepancies not only in poverty but also in escaping it. For example, African Americans are more likely than whites to be born into poverty and stay there. Many factors influence mobility, including education and employment.

Mobility appears to be declining. One study found that mobility decreased from the 1980s to the 2000s. Researchers suggested that increasing income inequality could be making it more difficult to move between rungs of the social ladder.

They say race distracts from the real issues. However, it is clear that race and class both remain important factors in people's lives. There continue to be discrepancies between races and classes when it comes to health, education, neighborhoods, crime, incarceration, and social mobility in the United States. Some people believe that acting as though race or class do not exist may be ultimately unhelpful and even harmful, because it attempts to ignore the important history and experiences of America's citizens.

Race and class add new insight when examining the meaning of the American dream. Although there is no universal definition of the American dream, it has traditionally referred to any citizen having an equal opportunity for success and social mobility. To those who advocate the American dream, all people need is to work hard and have personal responsibility. This is sometimes summed up by the phrase, "Pull yourself up by your bootstraps." History, however, shows that race and class shape experiences, challenges, and inequalities, putting the traditional American dream out of reach for some Americans.

Discussions of class and race play important roles in the way US society runs. Their significance continues to be debated as Americans elect leaders, welcome new immigrants, and face new challenges. Conversations about race and class also have an important role as people try to make society better. Modern movements such as Black Lives Matter have found the national spotlight, sparking both support and controversy. Looking back in the country's history shows that the ties between class and race run deep.

DISCUSSION STARTERS

- Do you think the response to the Flint water crisis would have been different if Flint were a wealthier city? Why or why not?

- Do class and race affect your everyday life? If so, how?

- Does your class or race influence how you think of yourself? If so, in what ways? If not, why?

- What does the American dream mean to you? Do you think people of different classes or races define the American dream differently? Do all classes and races have equal access to the American dream? Why or why not? Is the American dream alive today? Why or why not?

TWO

THIS LAND IS
OUR LAND

Native Americans have fought for centuries for their culture and land—and to be seen as equals in the American class system. Since Europeans first arrived, they aimed to obtain Native American land. The British colonies and then the US government isolated, displaced, and fought Native Americans to control this resource. Throughout the 1800s, the US government moved Native Americans to areas away from the rest of American society. These places often lacked natural resources. Sometimes Native Americans were pressured and gave up land through treaties. Other times, they were violently forced out.

As the United States expanded westward, its military detained Native Americans and forced them onto new lands.

CHEROKEE ASSIMILATION

After 1800, the Cherokee Nation assimilated to many American ways of life. Living in the southeastern United States, many of its people knew English and ran mills or ranches. They built houses, and white missionaries taught in their schools. In the 1820s, Sequoyah, a member of their tribe, created a Cherokee writing system using symbols for words. The system was easy to learn and spread quickly among the people.

Despite the Cherokees' assimilation, the government was not satisfied to let them remain on their traditional lands. According to historian Roger L. Nichols, "With educated leaders, growing economic strength, and widespread literacy, the tribe posed a major challenge to frontier politicians and land-hungry pioneers."[1]

To fight the 1830 Indian Removal Act, the Cherokee requested that the US Supreme Court intervene against the State of Georgia, but the court would not hear the case. The next year, however, the court ruled in the Cherokees' favor. President Andrew Jackson refused to enforce the ruling. The Cherokee people were moved thousands of miles from their traditional lands to Indian Territory, in present-day Oklahoma. The forced march became known as the Trail of Tears. More than 4,000 Cherokee died during the march.[2] Other nations forced to march in the Trail of Tears included the Chickasaw, Choctaw, Creek, and Seminole.

The Native American peoples themselves were seen as nuisances in the way of US expansion. The government referred to their presence as "the Indian problem." As more settlers streamed west, many Native Americans were driven off their land. Under President Andrew Jackson, the Indian Removal Act of 1830 moved most Native Americans living east of the Mississippi to west of the river. Those who didn't move voluntarily were driven off the land to small, isolated areas.

The US government kept control of Native Americans and took over their lands by creating regions known as reservations.

The Indian Appropriations Act of 1851 created the reservation system. Forced onto reservations, Native Americans could not practice their traditional ways of life, such as hunting, fishing, and gathering. They were not allowed to leave without permission.

FORCED ASSIMILATION

Native Americans were historically stereotyped and seen as inferior to the white population. Whites called them "uncivilized" or "savages." Besides displacing the tribes, the US government enacted other policies to strip away Native American culture and make Native peoples more like the white population. This is known as forced assimilation.

NATIVE AMERICAN CITIZENSHIP

Native Americans were not considered US citizens until 1924. With the Indian Citizenship Act, all Native Americans born in the United States were granted citizenship. However, some states did not give all Native Americans the right to vote until 1957.

Legislation aimed at integrating Native Americans into mainstream society was often damaging to the tribes. For instance, the 1887 Dawes Act carved up Native American tribal land, giving individual Native Americans small allotments. The idea was that this would make Native Americans assimilate with white culture. They would stay in one place as farmers, live in small family systems rather than clans, and no longer be loyal to their tribes. The act was ultimately a failure that harmed the tribes. Among other problems, much of the land was not favorable for farming, and the law opened more land to non-Native people. By 1900, the Dawes Act had reduced Native American lands from 138 million acres (56 million ha) in 1887 to 78 million acres (32 million ha).[3]

Another way the US government forced assimilation was through boarding schools. Boarding schools on and off reservations attempted to make Native American children assimilate into English-speaking society. Separated from their families, children had their hair cut and were often given new, non-Native names. They were forbidden from wearing traditional clothing, practicing their religions, or speaking their languages. They faced strict punishments for breaking those rules.

RESERVATIONS TODAY

Today, reservations are overseen by the US Bureau of Indian Affairs (BIA). Tribes are sovereign nations, which means they govern themselves. There are more than 320 federal Indian lands treated as Indian reservations in the United States today.[4] The largest is the Navajo Nation Reservation, stretching 16 million

Students at Native American boarding schools were forced to give up many aspects of their culture.

acres (6.5 million ha) across Arizona, New Mexico, and Utah.[6] Approximately one in three people who identify as only Native American or Alaska Native lives on a reservation or tribal lands.[7]

Reservations are important places of Native American culture, containing strong family and community ties. However, reservations are often concentrated areas of extreme poverty, unemployment, and high rates of alcoholism and drug abuse. Native Americans experience unemployment at almost double

Today, many Native Americans find ways to maintain and celebrate their traditional cultures.

the rate of the overall population. According to *US News & World Report*, more than one in four Native people live in poverty.[8] Even when they are similar to whites in age, sex, and education level, they have much lower odds of being employed than whites do.

Despite government assistance for food, education, and health, problems persist. Some researchers cite a history of displacement and isolation as causes of these challenges on reservations. According to Ron Haskins of the Brookings Institution, "If people aren't integrated into American society then it's very difficult to reach them and create the basis for economic opportunity and affluence."[9]

Isolation and limited socioeconomic opportunities may also contribute to the addiction and substance abuse crises on reservations. Native Americans have the highest rate of drug-related deaths among racial groups in the country. The National Institutes of Health reports that Native American youth have the highest rate of alcohol use disorders of any racial group in the United States. The issues extend to babies who are born with fetal alcohol syndrome and drug addictions.

Native American individuals and nations are working to improve conditions on reservations. Some are doing so through policy and legal action. For example, along with several US cities, tribes are suing large drug distributors and pharmaceutical companies. They allege that the companies have flooded the market with addictive drugs. Some tribes are combating issues from inside their communities with support groups, outreach and prevention programs, and education.

CERTIFYING RACE

Various Native American groups are recognized by the US government. The BIA issues an official document that certifies a person has a certain degree of Native American ancestry from the recognized community. This document is called Certificate of Degree of Indian Blood or Certificate of Degree of Alaska Native Blood. The document can be controversial because of its role in identifying race and excluding some who consider themselves Native American. The National Museum of the American Indian blog asks, "Does carrying a Certificate of Degree of Indian Blood (CDIB) make you Indian? Does being raised away from a reservation and not having traditional knowledge make a person less Indian? Does knowing your language make you more Indian?"[10] Each tribe has its own unique criteria for membership.

Some advocate for Native American peoples through media, such as magazines and websites, while others work for the preservation of culture, art, and language. Many call for better representation of Native Americans. Writing for *Indian Country Today* in 2015, tribal rights attorney Tara Houska turned the "Indian problem" phrase on its head. "There's an Indian problem in this country, and it's only gotten worse," she said. "Despite repeated efforts to eradicate the original peoples of these United States, we stubbornly endure."[11]

DISCUSSION STARTERS

- How did the settlers and US government view Native Americans? How did race and class affect their treatment of Native Americans?

- Why do you think reservations are important cultural centers for many Native Americans?

THREE

SLAVERY TO
CITIZENSHIP

n 1641, Massachusetts became the first New England colony to legalize slavery. Throughout the next two centuries, demand for enslaved people from Africa, and for their descendants, increased in North America. Millions were forced to work on tobacco and cotton plantations. Enslaved people were the lowest class of society, considered property rather than human beings.

Soon after the American Revolution (1775–1783) ended, Northern states abolished slavery. But America's growing status as a powerful empire continued to depend on the Southern states' economy, which was built on slave labor. An enslaved labor force was also used to build historical landmarks, such as the White House and the US Capitol. In the years leading up to the Civil War (1861–1865), a large portion of US wealth

In colonial America, enslaved people struggled to survive.

was invested in enslaved people. On January 1, 1863, President Abraham Lincoln signed the Emancipation Proclamation. The act declared approximately three million enslaved people in the South would be freed, though it had no practical effect until Union troops arrived in an area to enforce it. The proclamation applied only to regions that had seceded from the Union. Enslaved people in Union states were not freed. In May 1865, the Civil War ended in Union victory. In December, Congress ratified the Thirteenth Amendment to the US Constitution, which officially abolished slavery throughout the country.

The Union's victory reunited the country, but the bloody conflict had caused lasting divisions. Slavery was over, but for African Americans, the fight for full freedom and equal status was only beginning.

INDENTURED SERVANTS

In addition to slavery, the United States has a history of keeping indentured servants of various races. Until the 1700s, most Europeans arriving in America were indentured servants. This meant they had to work for years to pay off their passage, food, and shelter, often under harsh conditions. However, once their contract was up, they became free. They usually received a type of payment, such as land. They did not often rise high in society. The first African forced laborers in America were indentured servants before slave laws were passed. Indentured servitude eventually declined as slavery took hold.

GAINING AND LOSING

The Civil War was followed by a period known as Reconstruction (1865–1877), as the country worked to piece itself back together. Many African Americans left the South. They experienced some progress as they built lives as free people. They could participate in the political process, buy land, seek education, and work paid jobs. The Fourteenth Amendment, passed in 1868, affirmed the citizenship of African Americans and formerly enslaved people. It granted them equal legal and civil rights, protected under the Constitution. The Fifteenth Amendment, passed in 1870, allowed African American men to vote. African American women would not gain the same right until the passage of the Nineteenth Amendment in 1920 granted all women the right to vote.

THREE-FIFTHS COMPROMISE

Before the Civil War, an enslaved person was not counted as a full person under the US Constitution. At the Constitutional Convention of 1787, US delegates decided that the number of each state's representatives in the House of Representatives would be based on the state's population. However, Northern states were unsatisfied with the initial plan. Counting the Southern states' slave populations would lead to those states having more representatives, even though enslaved people could not vote. Delegates James Wilson and Roger Sherman proposed a solution known as the Three-Fifths Compromise. Under the compromise, enslaved people (described as "other Persons") were counted as three-fifths of a person.

As a result of America's rigid class system and racism, severe poverty persisted among African Americans following the end of slavery.

However, states of the former Confederacy immediately looked for ways around the new amendments to keep African Americans from rising in society. Southern states attempted to prevent African Americans from voting. States used violence, fraud, and poll taxes to suppress the vote. They also passed laws that made it difficult for African Americans to register to vote. Historians point to the failures of the Supreme Court and Congress to protect citizens' voting rights during this time.

EQUAL PROTECTION CLAUSE

The first section of the Fourteenth Amendment includes the equal protection clause. This clause means that states must treat individuals the same as others in similar circumstances. The 1954 US Supreme Court case *Brown v. Board of Education* was centered on the equal protection clause. The court's ruling declared racial segregation in public schools unconstitutional.

Beginning in the 1880s, states and cities passed laws to enforce segregation. These became known as Jim Crow laws, in reference to a stereotypical, insulting African American character popular in the 1800s. The regulations required separate schools, restaurants, public facilities, churches, hospital wards, parks, barbers, and more. African Americans were often relegated to facilities that were far inferior to those set aside for whites. By 1905, all states of the former Confederacy had implemented Jim Crow laws. Many laws would stand until the civil rights movement of the 1960s.

The system of sharecropping developed in the South during this time. In this system, poor whites and African Americans acted as land tenants, renting land from an owner for a share of the crop. According to historians Walda Katz Fishman and Jerome Scott, "Jim Crow and sharecropping were, in fact, an extension of a slightly modified slave system—economically, politically, and socially."[1] Southern farmers and sharecroppers experienced poverty, segregation, low-wage jobs, and poor education.

USING SCIENCE TO DISCRIMINATE

People have historically looked to science to support racist or discriminatory beliefs. In the 1920s, a popular movement took hold in the United States and other countries. Many well-educated and well-known people promoted the study of eugenics. Proponents of eugenics believed the human population could be improved by controlling genetics. The method of controlling genetics typically took the form of discrimination based on race, ethnicity, and physical ability. In 1920, Harry Laughlin, one of the leading advocates of eugenics, said that "the character of a nation is determined primarily by its racial qualities."[3]

Proponents encouraged practices such as selective breeding, which is the process of choosing parents with certain characteristics to have offspring. They believed that only people with desirable traits—mainly those considered fully white—should have children. Those with undesirable traits, such as the poor, immigrants, people of color, people with disabilities, and others, should not. These individuals were labeled as unfit or inferior. The government went so far as to sterilize people in more than two dozen US states.[4] Eugenics served to strengthen the ideas of white supremacists in the United States and around the world. Under Adolf Hitler, Nazi Germany enacted practices to eliminate Jews and others it believed inferior. The Nazis took inspiration from American eugenics in developing their own racist policies and forced-sterilization programs.

Meanwhile, a hateful movement was growing in popularity. In the 1920s, membership in the Ku Klux Klan, a white supremacist group, reached its all-time peak of four million.[2] It was the second rise of the Klan after its post–Civil War founding in 1865. The Klan had power and influence in many states, spreading messages of hate while inflicting violence and murder against African Americans. Group members also attacked immigrants, Jews, Catholics, and others who they didn't think conformed to American values.

CHANGING CLASSES

It can be easy for some Americans to forget about the inequalities of the past. Today, the gap has widened between the lowest and highest classes. This has made some people miss decades such as the 1950s, in which having a job and owning a home were signs of being part of the upwardly mobile middle class. However, historians point out that those times of postwar prosperity were also times of inequality for many. Richard Reeves of the Brookings Institution cautions, "We may not return to the jobs and families of the last century, and we may not want to, with the racial and gender inequality they concealed."[6]

LEFT OUT OF THE BOOM

During World War II (1939–1945), more than 2.5 million African Americans registered for the draft.[5] African Americans served with honor in both Europe and the Pacific, despite enduring segregated units and discrimination. Back home, others gained the opportunity to work in skilled jobs at wartime factories. However, African American soldiers returned home to the

Despite their service to the country, African American veterans were shut out of many of the rewards given to their white counterparts.

same unequal treatment they had experienced before. Despite serving their country, they remained in low social classes after the war. They still faced discriminatory laws and policies. They were the last hired and lowest paid, and they were again limited to low-skill positions. They were also left out of a key veterans' benefits bill that would have consequences for decades to come.

In 1944, President Franklin D. Roosevelt signed the Servicemen's Readjustment Act. Also known as the GI Bill, it provided benefits to war veterans returning home. These benefits ranged from college tuition payments to low-interest loans. The benefits helped veterans receive educations, start their own businesses, and buy homes or farms. Many of the GI Bill's recipients bought homes in newly created suburbs outside of large cities. As the postwar economy boomed and the United States became a world leader, the emergence of suburbs helped shape the United States' society, politics, and wealth.

African Americans were denied many of the GI Bill's benefits. Some African Americans were able to attend college, though in much lower numbers than their white peers. Many suburbs barred African Americans from moving in, denying them the opportunity to take part in the prosperous postwar lifestyle. Many African Americans instead stayed in the cities. They continued moving from the South to the North.

DISCUSSION STARTERS

- How did legislation such as the GI Bill help some Americans? How were other Americans left out?

- Do you think historical discrimination still affects society today? Why or why not?

FOUR

ALL IN THE
NEIGHBORHOOD

W here people live has the power to affect many other parts of their lives. Housing and neighborhoods play a role in how people live, who they interact with, how they raise children, what schools they attend, where they work, and what resources they can access. Housing has connections to educational achievement, health, and more.

Race and class are related to both housing and neighborhoods. Lower-income neighborhoods often do not have the same resources or quality of services as affluent areas. For instance, lower-income people more often live in areas that have fewer doctors, fewer opportunities for safe exercise, and fewer options for fresh foods. Schools for middle-class areas

Residents of lower-income neighborhoods may face challenges that people in wealthier parts of town do not have to deal with.

are 22 times more likely to be high achieving than those in low-income areas.[1]

Although the Civil Rights Act of 1964 outlawed legal segregation, divisions continue to exist between social classes and races throughout the United States. Residential segregation occurs when members of groups who share race, social class, age, or other characteristics live near one another and apart from other groups. Between 1970 and 2000, there was a significant rise in residential segregation. Segregation between whites and African Americans has proven to be significantly higher than segregation between social classes. Researchers point to the

COVENANTS OF CHICAGO

The famous 1940 US Supreme Court case *Hansberry v. Lee* centered on Chicago's restrictive housing covenants, or contracts about land use. Covenants had contributed to keeping the city's African American residents segregated for decades. The case involved the members of the Hansberry family, who were African American. Carl Hansberry had bought a house in an all-white neighborhood covered by a covenant that banned African Americans, and another homeowner sued to evict them. The lower court ruled that Hansberry could not argue against the neighborhood covenants because they had already been upheld in a prior court case.

The US Supreme Court reversed the lower court's decision on the basis that Hansberry was denied due process for class action lawsuits. The case inspired the play *A Raisin in the Sun*, written by Hansberry's daughter Lorraine. The play's title comes from a line in Langston Hughes's poem "Harlem." *Hansberry v. Lee* also led to another key court case, *Shelley v. Kraemer* (1948), which ruled that enforcing racially restrictive covenants is unconstitutional.

United States' complex history of racism and racial hostility as a factor in this.

Residential segregation is likely caused by a combination of factors. People may live near each other because of shared social class, as they may not be able to afford more expensive neighborhoods. Some groups who are poor may live in big cities with better access to public transportation and other resources. Others may choose to live near people they see as similar to themselves.

Prejudice and discrimination also cause segregation. The housing market has upheld many discriminatory practices that negatively affected African Americans, Hispanics, Asians, and other minority groups. By shutting African Americans out of suburbs throughout the 1940s and 1950s, the government contributed to decades of inequality. In some cases, minorities have been denied access to mortgages or treated as though they were unwelcome. Real estate agents sometimes direct people of certain races to or away from specific neighborhoods. Known as steering, this practice was made illegal in 1968. However, a 2006 report by the National Fair Housing Alliance found that realtors engaged in some form of steering during 87 percent of test encounters.[2] Additionally, major banks have recently been accused of illegally steering people into expensive or risky loans. In a 2017 lawsuit, the city of Philadelphia, Pennsylvania, accused

African American home buyers face fewer obstacles today than in the past, but discrimination still persists in some ways.

Wells Fargo of steering minority borrowers toward higher-cost and riskier mortgages than those offered to white home buyers.

HOUSING POLICIES

Government policies and agencies have played a role in housing segregation for decades. During the Great Depression, a severe economic downturn that persisted throughout the 1930s, many Americans lost their jobs and homes. Several federal housing programs with long-lasting effects were created as part of President Roosevelt's broad legislative response to the Depression, known as the New Deal. Although the New Deal programs led to benefits for some people, author Richard Rothstein argues that some of the programs contributed to a "state-sponsored system of segregation."[3]

Many policies centered around mortgages and loans that excluded people of color. The Home Owners' Loan Corporation was established in 1933. It helped homeowners avoid foreclosure by offering loans that were more affordable. However, this assistance did not apply to African American homeowners.

Another agency called the Federal Housing Administration (FHA) was established in 1934 under the National Housing Act. The FHA provided mortgage insurance on loans for first-time home buyers. However, many loans went to suburban areas rather than inner cities, where most African Americans lived. The FHA also subsidized builders of suburbs but required that the homes not be sold to African Americans, even if they could afford them. One FHA manual stated that "incompatible racial groups should not be permitted to live in the same communities."[4] According to the FHA, property values would decline if homes were sold to

BUCHANAN V. WARLEY

In 1917, the US Supreme Court made a landmark ruling in housing discrimination. In *Buchanan v. Warley*, a property owner in Louisville, Kentucky, refused to follow through on a purchase contract with an African American buyer. At the time, Louisville city ordinances did not allow African Americans to buy property in neighborhoods that were majority white and vice versa. The Supreme Court reversed the decisions of lower courts, unanimously ruling that the city ordinances were unconstitutional and went against the Fourteenth Amendment. Although both de facto and de jure segregation would continue, the case made it more difficult to pass other widespread segregation laws.

SUNSET TRAILER PARK

Not all white children grew up in the new suburbs of the 1950s. Allen Berube (1946–2007) was a historian and award-winning writer. In his essay "Sunset Trailer Park," coauthored with his mother, Berube explores the elements of race, class, and identity during his youth in a New Jersey trailer park. The park did not rent to African Americans. Even though some people looked down on the trailer park residents, Berube writes that Sunset had its own social classes and tensions. Sunset residents also tried proving to outsiders that they were higher class than others who lived there. "If we failed and fell to the bottom," Berube writes, "we were in danger of also losing, in the eyes of other white people, our claims to the racial privileges that came with being accepted as white Americans."[5]

African Americans, making loans too risky. However, there was no proof of this happening.

The Home Owners' Loan Corporation, FHA, and Veterans Administration began using a technique called redlining. In this practice, the government color coded maps of US metropolitan areas. The colors represented the safest places to insure mortgages. Neighborhoods with African American residents (or African Americans living nearby) were coded red. The color meant that the area was considered too risky for loans.

Other New Deal programs to address housing shortages included public housing for working-class families. Known as housing projects, the buildings were segregated. The projects eventually became subsidized housing for poor people. This meant that the government helped fund housing costs to keep rent affordable. While white middle- and lower-class families gained housing options and moved out of the cities and into mostly white suburbs, poor minorities were increasingly driven into inner-city housing projects. The phenomenon became known as white flight. It led to the formation of American ghettos. It also had long-term effects on class and race differences through generations. White families could use their home equity to send children to college, allowing them to accumulate wealth and take care of aging parents. Members of racial minorities, on the other hand, did not experience the same advantages.

DEVELOPMENT PROJECTS

Along with policies such as redlining and segregation, government programs of urban renewal helped form American ghettos. The Housing Act of 1949 enacted urban renewal programs, which provided cities with federal funds to buy, clear, and redevelop so-called slum neighborhoods. In places such as Detroit, thousands of people (mostly African American and low income) were displaced and left to search for housing. Oftentimes residents were displaced to areas that became slum neighborhoods, continuing the problem.

Many minority groups were affected by these redevelopment policies. In 1959 in Los Angeles, California, for example, thousands of Mexican Americans were forcibly cleared from the historic Bunker Hill neighborhood. Initially slated to be used for public housing, the land was eventually given to the Los Angeles Dodgers for a baseball stadium.

Government projects such as the 1950s interstate highway system also displaced minority residents. Newly built interstates in cities such as Syracuse, New York, were directed through the centers of minority neighborhoods. These served to break up African American communities and displace the residents.

Today, urban revitalization projects can be controversial. In some cases, an urban neighborhood is changed or renewed by more affluent people moving in. The process is known as gentrification. Some criticize gentrification as a force that displaces longtime low-income residents by raising housing and business costs. Others argue that gentrification improves public safety and quality of life.

SNOB ZONING

The Fair Housing Act of 1968 and later amendments have made it illegal to discriminate in housing based on race, color, age, sex, religion, disability, and other factors. The act in effect banned many practices that historically kept people of color from accessing housing, such as the refusal to rent or sell to people because of their race. It also made it illegal for realtors to lie about the availability of a house or apartment to keep a person of a certain race from buying it.

BLACK FLIGHT

African Americans have steadily been moving from city areas to suburbs for decades. Sometimes termed "black flight," this migration was especially notable in the early 2000s. Suburbs with majority African Americans are similar in many ways to their white counterparts. However, in 2016, as US home values rose, suburbs with majority African American residents did not experience the increase.

Under the Fair Housing Act, redlining and racial zoning are no longer allowed. However, in cities throughout the United States, local laws have the power to influence who moves into certain neighborhoods. By implementing certain types of zoning laws, neighborhoods can decide the economic status of their residents and, in effect, enforce racial and economic segregation.

Zoning that restricts residents based on status has become popularly known as "snob zoning." Some local zoning policies prevent companies from building apartments or having rental properties. Others require residential lots be a minimum size. Proponents of these policies say that the requirements are needed to maintain the look or character of the neighborhood. They assert that local governments should have the right to make zoning policies as they see fit and not be regulated by larger government authorities.

Critics argue that snob zoning has the same effect as racial zoning. They see it as a new way to keep out people of lesser status—and, by extension, people of color. Because minority groups do not have as much wealth as white people on average, the zoning laws tend to keep them out of neighborhoods. Snob zoning may also pose challenges to upward mobility for lower-income people and contribute to the cycle of poverty. As a result, some believe class is becoming the defining factor in the makeup of neighborhoods.

Several states are addressing the issue through new zoning policies. They require builders to make a percentage of housing developments affordable to low-income residents. Some people are calling on the government to implement reforms that are more wide ranging. According to researcher Richard Rothstein, "The truth is that segregation in every metropolitan area was imposed by racially explicit federal, state, and local policy, without which private actions of prejudice or discrimination would not have been very effective."[6] Rothstein adds that because the government helped create the problem, the government should be able to fix it.

DISCUSSION STARTERS

- How do you think historic housing policies shaped housing patterns today?

- How is residential segregation harmful to the affected residents?

- Do you see residential segregation where you live? If so, in what ways?

FIVE

THE CHANGING FACE
OF AMERICA

The population of the United States looks much different today than it did 50 years ago. Its residents are more racially and ethnically diverse than ever. Between 1965 and 2015, the percentage of non-Hispanic whites declined from 84 percent to 62 percent.[1] At the same time, the numbers of Americans who were either Hispanic or Asian increased.

Immigration is one of the principal reasons for the changing face of America. The United States has the largest immigrant population in the world. In 2015, immigrants made up 13.5 percent of the total US population.[2] The majority of today's immigrants come from Asia and Latin America.

Every year, thousands of immigrants from all over the world are naturalized as US citizens.

OPENING THE DOOR

The Immigration and Nationality Act of 1965, meant to end discriminatory immigration practices, paved the way for modern immigration. It changed quotas based on immigrant origins, which had favored European countries rather than those in Asia, Africa, and the Middle East. It also set up a system based on the immigrant's skills and his or her family relationships with US citizens. The law created the structure of immigration law that still exists today. Approximately 59 million immigrants have arrived since the law's passage.[4]

At the time of signing, President Lyndon B. Johnson, members of his administration, and other politicians did not predict the far-reaching effects the bill would have on American immigration and demographics for decades to come. "The bill that we sign today is not a revolutionary bill," said President Johnson. Senator Ted Kennedy added, "It will not upset the ethnic mix of our society."[5] The bill's many critics included conservative activist Myra C. Hacker, who shared sentiments still referenced by immigration critics today. She testified, "We should remember that people accustomed to such marginal existence in their own land will tend to live fully here, to hoard our bounteous minimum wages and our humanitarian welfare handouts . . . lower our wage and living standards, [and] disrupt our cultural patterns."[6]

NEW ARRIVALS

Social class plays a role in immigrants' lives before and after their arrival in the United States. According to researcher Oksana Yakushko, "Social class permeates all aspects of immigration. It often is a definitive cause of decisions to relocate. It is at the heart of the hope and struggle of immigrants after their move to a new country."[3]

Immigrants arrive with various backgrounds and varying levels of education and skills. Some immigrants may experience a reversal of social class after arriving in the United States. For instance, an immigrant may have had a respected career in her home country but arrive in the United States with fewer resources and lower social status. According to the 2010 US Census, foreign-born individuals are more likely to be in poverty than people who were born in the United States. Immigrants may face prejudice and discrimination, particularly from those who fear immigrants will not assimilate and will corrupt the American way of life. Despite the challenges, many immigrants find success in their new home.

Conversations on immigration challenges and inequality will be important as US demographics continue to evolve in the future. By the year 2065, the United States will be home to an estimated 78 million immigrants.[7] The success of immigrants in areas such as education and employment will shape the future of American life and neighborhoods. Some researchers suggest it could be helpful for teachers and mental health professionals to learn about the complex role of social class in immigrants' lives.

CHINESE EXCLUSION ACT

Throughout the 1850s, Chinese immigrants arrived in the western United States to work in railroad construction, agriculture, factories, and gold mines. As they became successful and started their own businesses, prejudice grew. The Chinese Exclusion Act of 1882 stopped Chinese immigration to the United States and banned Chinese people from becoming US citizens. The act was repealed in 1943, but only a small number of Chinese immigrants were allowed annually until passage of the Immigration and Nationality Act of 1965.

IRISH
IMMIGRANTS

People of Irish descent in the United States were once considered a separate race from other Europeans. In 1845, the people of Ireland were starving after a potato disease wiped out the nation's key crop. Nearly two million people (a quarter of the entire population of Ireland) made their way to the United States. On arrival, they were largely scorned because of their origin, poverty, and Catholicism. Viewed as disease-ridden criminals, they were met with mobs, violence, and discrimination. Newspaper ads for employment went so far as to say, "No Irish Need Apply."

Irish were not considered to be white. Author Noel Ignatiev writes, "While the white skin made the Irish eligible for membership in the white race, it did not guarantee their admission; they had to earn it."[8] Irish were seen to be similar to free African Americans, with common social classes, jobs, and neighborhoods. Although oppressed themselves, many Irish soon discovered they could distance themselves from African Americans to improve their opportunities for success. Consequently, the Irish rose in status by helping to oppress groups such as African Americans and Chinese. Irish immigrants began gaining a foothold in upper social classes by the late 1800s.

Contemporary newspaper editorial drawings illustrated the plight of people coming from extreme poverty in Ireland.

HARPER'S WEEKLY.

JOURNAL OF CIVILIZATION.

Vol. XXIV.—No. 1209.]

NEW YORK, SATURDAY, FEBRUARY 28, 1880.

Entered according to Act of Congress, in the Year 1880, by Harper & Brothers, in the Office of the Librarian of Congress, at Washington.

SINGLE COPIES TEN CENTS.
$4.00 PER YEAR IN ADVANCE.

THE HERALD OF RELIEF FROM AMERICA.

Immigrants' rights organizations and their supporters believe in immigration policies that are less harsh and more sympathetic to the challenges immigrants face.

Understanding social class, along with culture and other factors, could help in providing care and services to immigrant populations. It could also help inform efforts to fight for immigrant rights and equality.

Refugees make up another group of new arrivals. These are individuals who are forced to leave their home country to escape war, persecution, or violence. The United States has historically been the world leader in resettling refugees. According to the US State Department, more than three million refugees have arrived in the United States since 1975.[9] Most refugees come from the Middle East, Asia, and Africa. After being vetted, they are eligible for monetary assistance, language classes, and job training. The president consults with Congress to determine the maximum number of refugees allowed in each year. In September 2017, President Donald Trump's administration announced a record-low cap of 45,000 refugees, approximately half the number allowed by the previous administration.[10]

UNDOCUMENTED IMMIGRANTS

One group of immigrants has unique social and economic challenges to succeeding in the United States. Undocumented immigrants are those who enter the country without legal permission. In 2015, an estimated 11 million undocumented immigrants lived in the United States.[11] Undocumented immigrants may take low-paying jobs without benefits or insurance. They are also more likely to be exploited because they do not have legal protections. They may fear being detected and deported by the authorities if they report a crime. In many states, an undocumented immigrant cannot obtain a driver's license and may have a difficult time opening a bank account. Undocumented immigrants cannot receive federal aid and are legally not allowed to receive benefits such as welfare. Still, they must report income and pay taxes. According to a Social Security Administration study, undocumented immigrants paid as much as $13 billion in Social Security taxes in 2010.[12] The challenges of being undocumented also make it difficult for the next generation to rise in status.

A growing number of researchers advocate the importance of intersectionality when studying immigration. Intersectionality is the idea that social categories overlap and affect an individual's experience of oppression. For example, researcher Kevin Johnson takes both class and race into account when examining immigration law and enforcement. He writes that US immigration laws have been constructed to keep out poor and working people of color, pointing out, "Immigration law expressly defines who can and cannot enter the United States and, not surprisingly, mirrors the class and racial hierarchies that exist in American society."[13] Johnson adds that class and race can also play roles in stereotypes of immigrants as poor and unskilled and are present in negative terms such as "illegal aliens."[14]

Debate continues to rage over undocumented immigration. Some call for the deportation of undocumented individuals, believing these people are competing with US citizens for low-skill jobs. Others press for reforms that would create paths to citizenship for those who are already living and working in the United States.

DREAMERS

The Deferred Action for Childhood Arrivals (DACA) program was a government initiative that prevented the deportation of individuals who were brought to the United States illegally as minors. Participants could obtain a two-year, renewable deferment from deportation. President Obama created the program in 2012. The people affected by the program are commonly known as Dreamers. An estimated 800,000 of them applied to DACA in the years following the program's creation.[16]

Advocates said that DACA provided economic opportunities for qualifying individuals as they received work permits, opened bank accounts, received driver's licenses, and went to school. These things, in turn, benefited the US economy as a whole. A 2016 study found that DACA reduced the likelihood of poverty in households headed by Dreamers by 38 percent.[17] However, the program offered neither a path to citizenship nor the comprehensive immigration reform that lawmakers had been promising for years. Conservatives accused Obama of executive overreach because he created the program through an executive order.

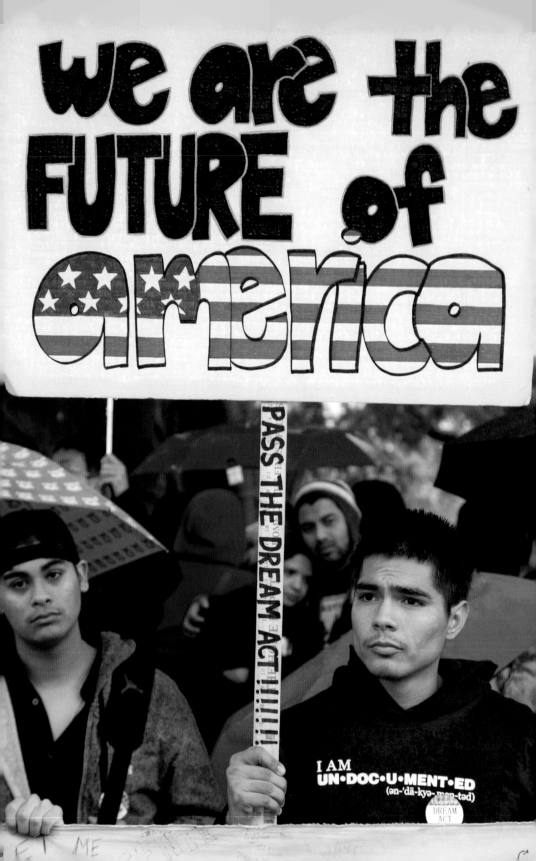

In 2017, the Trump administration announced that the program would be ending the following year. Trump called on Congress to come up with a new immigration plan. Although some decried the move as cruel to the Dreamers, others agreed that Congress was rightfully responsible for passing legislation on this issue. They blamed Congress for its previous failures to act and called on lawmakers for a solution. The *Economist* pointed out that most DACA recipients were high achievers who were employed. Many were business owners, and many were married to American citizens and had children of their own. "They are American in every sense bar the bureaucratic one," the newspaper wrote. "Correcting that should be about as hard politically as declaring a new public holiday."[18]

DISCUSSION STARTERS

- Have you seen or experienced the effects of immigration?

- What challenges do you think immigrants might experience coming to the United States? How might this affect their social status? How might a refugee's experience be different from that of someone who immigrated for another reason?

- What do you think about the debate between those who call for undocumented immigrants to be deported and those who believe they should be given a path to citizenship?

SIX

CLOSING
THE GAPS

G aps between the classes are widening. In 1983, the top 10 percent of households controlled approximately 68.2 percent of the wealth in the country. By 2007, those households controlled 73 percent of the wealth.[1] Among races, the income gap between African American and white households has also increased since the 1980s. The gap between Hispanic and white households has remained large as well. Gaps have increased in the workplace, too. While corporate executives made 24 times as much as average employees in 1965, they made 185 times more by 2009.[2]

The achievement gap refers to the differences in educational outcomes among different groups of US students, such as boys

Large corporations are more prosperous than ever, but that new wealth has not reached lower-income families.

BRIDGING THE TECHNOLOGY GAP

In a world that is increasingly run by technology, having access to the internet and digital devices is important. Technology has become a facet of daily life in homes, schools, and workplaces. The term *digital divide* is used to refer to the gap in technology access between groups of individuals.

A 2016 report found that most low- and moderate-income families have some type of internet connection. However, many are "under-connected," meaning they have unreliable or limited access. The report's researchers wrote that the issue of inequality would be solved only by a collective effort. According to the researchers, "The solution to this challenge will require innovative partnerships and new commitments aligning government, industry, education, and community leaders—including families themselves."[4]

and girls, whites and racial minorities, or students from varying income backgrounds. Test scores are an example of a way to measure educational outcome. Educational gaps in areas such as test scores have historically been found to exist because of unequal educational opportunities. Researchers have continually studied the disparities between groups of students and tried to come up with solutions.

A 2016 study analyzed American adults' opinions about test score gaps between groups of students. The researchers concluded that the public was more concerned about the gaps between rich and poor than they were about gaps having to do with the students' race or ethnicity. They found that 36 percent of American adults saw it as essential or high priority to close the gap between white and African American students. However, 64 percent said the same about the gap between poor and wealthy students.[3]

As various gaps increase, so do inequalities in health, resources, and quality of life. Researchers use socioeconomic status (SES) to measure a combination of factors including a person's income, education, financial security, and his or her perceptions of social status. A low SES reflects such things as poverty, low educational level, and poor health. According to the American Psychological Association, race and ethnicity are tied to a person's SES. Racial and ethnic minorities experience disparities in discrimination, educational outcomes, health care, and psychological stress.

EFFECTS OF POVERTY

Poverty goes deeper than having little money and few material goods. It has far-reaching consequences, including homelessness, stress, isolation, hunger, and illness. People of different races experience poverty differently. For example, African Americans are more likely than white Americans to experience concentrated poverty.

KING CALLS FOR EQUALITY

Civil rights leader Martin Luther King Jr. believed that racial equality would be possible only with economic equality. King called for people of all races to come together to fight for economic and political power. In 1967, King remarked, "Negroes are not the only poor in the nation. There are nearly twice as many white poor as Negro, and therefore the struggle against poverty is not involved solely with color or racial discrimination but with elementary economic justice."[5] A year later, King was in Memphis, Tennessee, to support striking African American sanitation workers, when he was assassinated.

OCCUPY
WALL STREET

From September 17, 2011, to November 15, 2011, activists took over New York City's Zuccotti Park. Rallied around a feeling of anger toward corporate greed and power, they were protesting the widening gap between the few wealthy Americans and the many poor and middle-class Americans. Activists decried the small group of the most-wealthy people as "the one percent" who controlled much of the US economic system.[6]

The movement became known as Occupy Wall Street. Drawing both supporters and critics, it inspired similar protests around the world. People of many races participated, concerned about high unemployment and soaring student loan debt. The movement gained critics within its own ranks, who charged that the protesters ignored some voices as they single-mindedly pursued economic equality. These critics argued that in order to be a true movement of change, Occupy Wall Street needed to recognize how corporate greed was connected to social structures such as racism. Activist Manissa Maharawal pointed out, "We are the 99 percent, but the way that we experience the 99 percent can be very different."[7] To people such as Maharawal, the movement would only be successful at creating change if it were inclusive, recognizing the experiences of different backgrounds and privileges. It had to be different from the system they were trying to overcome together.

Occupy Wall Street protesters spoke against the greed and misdeeds of corporations.

This means they live clustered in areas of poverty. Concentrated poverty exists in cities across the country, in areas of Appalachia, on Native American reservations, and in other communities. Areas of concentrated poverty can create what is known as the "double burden" of poverty, meaning people experience not only the negative effects of their own poverty but also those of the poverty around them. For example, a person who is poor and also lives in a poor neighborhood deals with additional disadvantages such as high crime rates and low-quality educational opportunities. The person may experience health risks because of overcrowded housing or unsanitary conditions.

Although poverty in the United States has always affected people of all races, it disproportionately affects racial minorities. In 2014, the percentages of African American and Latino youth living in poverty were more than double the rates for white, non-Latino, and Asian youth. There are more whites in poverty than members of other racial groups, but whites' overall rate of poverty is lower. In addition, poverty rates among immigrants are significantly higher than those of nonimmigrants.

GOVERNMENT SOCIAL PROGRAMS

The US government has created various programs to assist citizens by providing basic income, educational assistance and training, food and housing security, health care, and emergency relief. Several social welfare programs were implemented as part of the wider civil rights reform in the 1960s. President

Lyndon B. Johnson's War on Poverty initiative promised to give impoverished citizens "a hand up, not a handout."[8] Among other efforts in areas such as food and education, the initiative created Medicare, a health insurance program that provides coverage to people ages 65 and older, and Medicaid, a program that provides free health insurance for people who have low income.

Government welfare refers to government assistance for citizens who have low income. The present-day Temporary Assistance to Needy Families program provides cash benefits to very low-income families with children. It also helps adults become and stay employed. Another program, called the Supplemental Nutrition Assistance Program (SNAP), provides income support to qualifying individuals and is the country's largest food-assistance program.

The effectiveness of Johnson's programs and modern welfare policies on poverty in the United States continues to be debated.

HIRING BY NAME?

In 2003, a National Bureau of Economic Research study famously asked, "Are Emily and Greg More Employable than Lakisha and Jamal?" The study authors submitted resumes under fake names that were traditionally associated with either whites or African Americans. They found that the resumes with "white-sounding" names received significantly more callbacks. "Differential treatment by race still appears to be prominent in the labor market," the group concluded.[9] Several similar studies have been done since, with some suggesting racial discrimination based on names is less prevalent.

The War on Poverty launched by President Johnson, *speaking*, led to the creation of several programs designed to assist lower-income Americans.

Some conservative critics say the War on Poverty was a failure that has decreased recipients' self-sufficiency while ineffectively spending government funds. They say welfare's current state makes people dependent on it, leading to cycles of social problems. Others contend that many of the initiatives continue to offer essential benefits and assist in giving people the needed "hand up" on the road to a more equitable society.

Several studies have examined the public's attitudes about government welfare in the United States, as well as people's perceptions about who receives the assistance. A 2016 study found that people tend to picture African Americans and negative stereotypes when thinking of welfare recipients. The study's authors pointed out that this was despite African Americans making up only approximately one-third of the programs' recipients. The results suggested that people's mental images of welfare recipients could lead to bias in welfare support.

EXAMINING AFFIRMATIVE ACTION

The social reform of the civil rights movement led to the creation of affirmative action programs and policies. Affirmative action aims to improve opportunities for groups that have been discriminated against in the past. It often relates to educational or employment policies, such as in college admissions or job hiring.

A 1961 executive order by President John F. Kennedy marked a new era in the federal government's efforts to advance equal opportunity. Executive Order 10925 established what is now known as the US Equal Employment Opportunity Commission. Today, the commission enforces federal laws that prevent workplace discrimination.

COMBATING POVERTY

President Johnson's War on Poverty initiative included the Food Stamp Act of 1964, which eventually led to the present-day SNAP. The Economic Opportunity Act of 1964 led to the creation of the Job Corps, which offers employment training. It also led to Head Start, which supports early childhood education, and the Volunteers in Service to America program, which works to end poverty through community projects such as job skill training, youth mentoring, and veteran homelessness prevention. The Elementary and Secondary Education Act created the Title I program, which provides funding to school districts with large populations of low-income students.

Affirmative action policies can create college campuses that are more diverse.

President Kennedy's executive order also gave the first directive for affirmative action. Kennedy ordered that government contractors "take affirmative action to ensure that applicants are employed, and that employees are treated during employment, without regard to their race, creed, color or national origin."[10] The order also allowed federal contracting agencies to implement penalties against contractors who did not follow the requirements.

Since its inception, affirmative action has garnered equally fierce supporters and critics. Advocates of affirmative action in college admissions say the policies will help groups that have been left behind and left out in the past. They say the policies help level the playing field and foster diversity. They point to the increased enrollment and economic opportunities the programs afford to low-income or minority students.

Critics see educational affirmative action as outdated, unneeded, and unfair. Some call it a form of reverse discrimination. They believe it admits less-qualified students from minority groups instead of more-qualified white students. They also question the benefits to students from the lowest economic background because some studies show the policies generally benefit middle- and upper-class minority students. Others say allowing in underqualified students leads to a situation in which the students are set up for failure. Some critics say affirmative action policies are insulting to the groups at which they are directed because they imply the individuals need special forms of assistance to succeed.

DISCUSSION STARTERS

- What do you think about the United States' distribution of wealth between wealthy and poor? What other information would you like to learn about this?

- What do you think about affirmative action? Is it fair or unfair? What are the arguments of the other side? Do you think these types of programs are needed in the United States today? Why or why not?

SEVEN

LAW
ENFORCEMENT

I n 2014, the city of Ferguson, Missouri, became the focus of a national debate over race, class, and policing. On August 9, an 18-year-old African American man named Michael Brown was shot to death in the street by a white police officer. Unrest immediately followed, with thousands participating in vigils and months-long protests. Activists and community leaders arrived in Ferguson, including those from a group called Black Lives Matter. They chanted, "Whose streets? Our streets," "No justice, no peace," and "Hands up, don't shoot."[1]

Some demonstrations turned violent, and riots erupted with looting and vandalism. National Guard troops were deployed to the city. Police used tear gas, rubber bullets, and military

Police and activists came into conflict during the protests that followed the shooting of Michael Brown in Ferguson, Missouri.

equipment on peaceful protesters and the media, inflaming nationwide protests over police bias. A grand jury later declined to charge the officer who shot Brown with a crime.

A subsequent investigation by the US Department of Justice found widespread racial bias and a "predatory system of government" in the Ferguson Police Department and court system that particularly targeted poor, black residents.[2] Some of the unfair treatment included fees and fines for minor offenses that resulted in jail time if not paid. One researcher remarked that the fees "served as the gateway for an elaborate poverty trap for citizens, who became mired in cycles of perpetual debt and payment and mounting entanglements with police and courts."[3] Similar reports of systematic racial bias appeared in cities across the United States, causing many to question the accountability of police.

As people continue to examine police shootings in closer detail than ever before, they offer varying theories as to why police decide to shoot.

POWER OF MEDIA

Media coverage of the unrest in Ferguson highlights the power of language in shaping opinions. For instance, media outlets referred to 18-year-old Michael Brown in various terms, calling him a "kid," "teenager," "man," "thug," or "criminal." Each could serve to paint a different picture of the individual. Researchers point out that words such as *thug* work as a type of racially coded language. In the same way, even peaceful protesters were variously depicted as vigilantes, rioters, or members of an angry street mob. By presenting a biased account, a media outlet can sow more tension and division.

Writing for the *Week*, Damon Linker held that class, not race, was the root problem. "America has a serious problem with police violence—but its victims are not just African Americans. The victims are those—whether white, black, Hispanic, or 'other'—who reside far from the top of the socioeconomic pyramid," he writes. "However bad our race problem is and remains, our class problems may be even bigger."[4]

POLICING THE POLICE

Throughout the 1970s and 1980s, new, aggressive police methods were implemented across the United States. These changes came after political unrest in the 1960s and 1970s. New focus was placed on local police operations. President Johnson declared, "The front-line soldier in the war on crime is the local law enforcement officer."[5] In 1965, Congress passed the Law Enforcement Assistance Act, which gave the federal government a direct role in local policing,

OVERLOOKING CLASS

In a 2014 *Time* magazine opinion article, former pro basketball player Kareem Abdul-Jabbar states that focusing on the racial aspect of the Michael Brown shooting takes away from a bigger issue, writing, "Of course, to many in America, being a person of color is synonymous with being poor, and being poor is synonymous with being a criminal." He writes of a largely ignored police shooting in 1970 in Mississippi, adding, "Unless we want the Ferguson atrocity to also be swallowed and become nothing more than an intestinal irritant to history, we have to address the situation not just as another act of systemic racism, but as what else it is: class warfare."[6]

INCARCERATION RATES

The United States has the highest incarceration rate in the world. The country incarcerates 716 people for every 100,000. In some individual states, the rate is much higher, with Louisiana incarcerating 1,341 for every 100,000. For global comparison, the next highest country is Cuba, with 510 per 100,000.[7]

Since the 1970s, changing policies, including the war on drugs, have led to high rates of incarceration. This mass incarceration points to stark disparities between classes and races. Members of racial minorities make up the majority of prisoners. Particularly, young African American men with little education are disproportionately likely to be incarcerated. Native American youth are also incarcerated at a high rate. Researchers have pointed out that mass incarceration affects people who were already disadvantaged, contributing to generational cycles of poverty and other disadvantages. Critics continue to call for reforms to policies that lead to mass incarcerations, attesting that incarceration does not effectively reduce crime. They suggest finding alternative ways to correct social problems. Many also criticize the boom in prison construction for hindering sentencing reform. Between 1970 and 2000, the number of US prisons increased from 511 to more than 1,600. Approximately 70 percent of prisons have been built in rural areas, where they offer boosts to local economies.[8]

courts, and prisons. It also established funding for military-level police equipment. It helped lead to the 1968 establishment of the Law Enforcement Assistance Administration, which directed federal funding to law enforcement and crime programs. Although Johnson's War on Poverty continued its focus on creating social welfare programs and policies, crime proved to be the more popular issue. "Over time, national policymakers retreated from and eventually dismantled many of the social welfare programs of [Johnson's initiatives]," says researcher Elizabeth Hinton. "The War on Crime, on the other hand, became the foremost policy approach to the social and demographic challenges of the late twentieth century."[9]

As the size and power of police forces grew, use of force and rates of arrest increased as police looked to curb crimes on the street level. Studies showed that certain communities were targeted. According to researchers Joe Soss and Vesla Weaver, "High-volume stops and low-level arrests were weakly correlated with crime but showed a strong connection to race, poverty, and place."[10] African Americans were more likely to be stopped but less likely to have evidence of wrongdoing. Critics believe policing has functioned as a type of social regulation, focusing on people in poorer neighborhoods with less power.

Spurred on by high-profile incidents such as Ferguson, police reforms have begun to take place, with many departments focusing on improving policies, strengthening community relationships, and creating better training for officers. Some departments have made concerted efforts to build trust with members of poorer communities. Trust has been shown to make police more effective, as community members who trust law enforcement will be more likely to call the police, report crimes, and cooperate with officers.

WAR ON DRUGS

The expansion of US police forces coincided with the government's war on drugs that continues today. In 1971,

President Richard Nixon declared war on drugs, calling drug abuse "public enemy number one."[11] Throughout the 1970s and 1980s, the United States began imposing new drug laws. Expanded street level policing dramatically increased drug arrests and incarcerations, even for low-level offenses. Although some politicians and community members praised the efforts as making streets safer, others have said these practices have led to reinforcement of stereotypes because, they believed, the poor and people of color were more likely to be viewed as criminals.

Some police departments have sent officers out into neighborhoods to meet with residents, hoping to improve trust between law enforcement and the community.

As drug arrests have continued to increase, so have their racial disparities. Although African Americans are not more likely to use drugs than whites, they are six to ten times more likely to be incarcerated for drug offenses.[12] A 2015 study found that African Americans were 247 percent more likely and Hispanics 60 percent more likely than whites to experience a drug distribution arrest by age 29.[13] To try to lessen the disparity, several cities have recently begun adopting policies that would make low-level drug offenses, such as nonviolent marijuana possession, lower priorities for arrest. Many hope that these types of drug policy reforms will help reduce racial disparities in arrests and prison sentences.

ENFORCING DRUG LAWS

The war on drugs saw the 1973 creation of the US Drug Enforcement Agency (DEA). According to Nixon, the need was urgent. "Right now, the federal government is fighting the war on drug abuse under a distinct handicap, for its efforts are those of a loosely confederated alliance facing a resourceful, elusive, worldwide enemy," he said. "Certainly, the cold-blooded underworld networks that funnel narcotics from suppliers all over the world are no respecters of the bureaucratic dividing lines that now complicate our anti-drug efforts."[14] Today, the DEA continues its mission to prevent drug trafficking and use.

OPIOIDS OUT OF CONTROL

Beginning in the 1990s, abuse of prescription opioids increased sharply, particularly among white users. By 2010, many had turned to the opioid heroin, which had previously been viewed

Needles used for taking opioids sit out in the open along a riverbank in Massachusetts.

as a problem of the African American community. In 2015, 90 percent of the total opioid and heroin deaths were among whites.[15] In 2016, more than 59,000 people died.[16]

In 2017, President Trump called on the Department of Health and Human Services to declare the opioid crisis a public health emergency. This would expand some funding and services.

The opioid issue was an important one to his working-class white supporters. Advocacy groups continued to call for more drastic action.

Meanwhile, debate broke out over the portrayal of opioid abuse and deaths. Whereas the opioid crisis was treated as a health epidemic requiring treatment and funding, addiction issues common in minority communities have been historically ignored or criminalized. Many saw the influence of race in the response to the drug problem. "Look at the inner city; it's always been what we consider an epidemic," said a Memphis pastor. "If this had been the case in other areas, the community would have been crying out long ago. But now that it's taking the lives of European-Americans, we find that it's at a time of crisis."[17]

DISCUSSION STARTERS

- Do you think racism has played a role in the war on drugs? Why or why not? How about class discrimination?

- How might people's race and class influence how they are portrayed in the media after an encounter with police?

- How can the media contribute to bias? Can you think of some ways to spot media bias having to do with class or race?

EIGHT

POLITICS AND
POWER

The Democratic and Republican parties have dominated US politics for more than 150 years. In 2016, the Pew Research Center found large differences in party affiliation among races. Among African American voters, an overwhelming 87 percent have Democratic leanings.[1] Both Hispanic and Asian voters also lean Democratic. In recent years, white voters have increasingly leaned Republican.

The class and race alignments of these two primary political parties have shifted throughout the past centuries. In the post–Civil War South, the Democratic Party was responsible for passing Jim Crow laws and suppressing the African American vote. Known as the "Solid South," the South would remain firmly Democratic until the civil rights era of the 1960s. During the

Political parties have long tried to use divisions of class and race to their advantage.

Great Depression, the New Deal policies of President Roosevelt, a Democrat, appealed to many voters affected by unemployment and poverty, including African Americans and Southern whites. Many African Americans switched their party allegiance to the Democratic party in the 1930s. By the civil rights era of the 1960s, Democrats began calling for policies improving gender and racial equality while the Republican Party grew increasingly conservative.

SOUTHERN STRATEGY

The phrase *Southern Strategy* refers to the Republican Party's successful tactics to secure the votes of Southern states that had previously been solidly Democratic. The strategy began with Republican Barry Goldwater's 1964 promotion of states' rights as reason to oppose the Civil Rights Act. The idea of states' rights means leaving political decisions up to individual states rather than the federal government. Many view the Southern Strategy as appealing to voters' racist attitudes, although both the strategy and its effects have continued to be debated. Some political scientists have contended that the Southern voting shift from Democratic to Republican occurred because of economics, not race.

CONTROLLING THE VOTES

When it comes to voter participation, deep divides exist between classes. Research continually finds that people with lower incomes or less education are generally less engaged in politics. They do not vote, talk about politics, or give political donations as often as people with more resources. Some reasons for this may be that they do not believe they

THE KERNER COMMISSION

In the mid-1960s, racial unrest came to a head as riots broke out in several major US cities, including Chicago, Illinois; Newark, New Jersey; Atlanta, Georgia; Tampa, Florida; Los Angeles, California; and Detroit, Michigan. In 1967, President Johnson formed a National Commission on Civil Disorders to investigate the causes of the riots and how they could be prevented from happening again. Led by Illinois governor Otto Kerner, the bipartisan group became known as the Kerner Commission.

The commission's report was released in early 1968 and became a best seller. It concluded that the violence was caused by white racism, stating, "White racism is essentially responsible for the explosive mixture which has been accumulating in our cities since the end of World War II."[2] According to the report, racist structures in society led to poor conditions for African Americans and feelings of frustration at lack of economic opportunity.

The report cited employment discrimination, residential segregation, increasing poverty, and feelings of powerlessness in the African American community. The commission's recommendations included creating housing, education, employment, and welfare programs. It also recommended improved police training and treatment of African American citizens. The report stated, "Our nation is moving toward two societies, one black, one white—separate and unequal."[3] In 2018, former senator Fred Harris, the only living member of the Kerner Commission, worked with a group that revisited the commission's goals and compared them to the country's progress. They found many areas to be unimproved, such as racial injustice and poverty, and made their own recommendations for change.

can influence change or that they think they are not welcome to participate.

When race is taken into consideration, in recent elections African Americans have usually had lower voter turnout than whites. Latinos and Asian Americans have had still lower rates of voter turnout. Researcher Daniel Laurison points out that a group's lower political participation means that its opinions are less likely to be considered, calling it "one more way that people with the least resources and power in our society are shut out of meaningful participation in our collective life."[4]

Money also influences politics. US political campaigns are often financed by wealthy individuals and political action committees (PACs) formed by corporations, labor unions, or other organizations. A new type of PAC, known as a Super PAC, was made possible following 2010 court decisions. These types of PACs can raise unlimited amounts of money from individuals as long as they do not directly coordinate with a candidate on how to spend the funds. This means that individuals can give millions of dollars to such groups. Normally, campaign contributions are limited to a few thousand dollars per individual. Proponents of campaign finance reform say that less wealthy individuals do not have the same power as wealthy individuals to influence candidates and elections. Others hold that even small donations can add up to make a difference for a political candidate.

Political leaders may influence the power of a vote. In the controversial practice of gerrymandering, legislators redraw the boundaries of their electoral districts to give advantage to one party or the other. They may draw the lines to put groups of voters together in a small area ("packing"), or separate groups of voters to dilute their votes' power ("cracking"). Both tactics were present in a 2017 Supreme Court case regarding North Carolina gerrymandering that had occurred in 2011. The state's

Many citizens have strongly protested against the process of gerrymandering.

Republican lawmakers redrew the district boundaries in ways that packed African Americans into one district and weakened their voting power in another. The Supreme Court ruled this effort unconstitutional as racially motivated gerrymandering.

In recent years, several election practices have come under fire and have been struck down in court for being discriminatory. Many have been accused of suppressing the votes of those in poorer communities or people of color. Controversial voting laws include those that require types of identification to vote and those that limit early and absentee voting. Supporters of voter ID laws say that the practice protects against voter fraud.

SHELBY COUNTY V. HOLDER

In 2013, the US Supreme Court struck down part of the 1965 Voting Rights Act in a 5–4 vote in the case *Shelby County v. Holder*. The act had originally required states with a history of discrimination to get federal approval before changing their voting laws. The 2013 decision removed that requirement. Chief Justice John Roberts wrote that the original act no longer reflected current voting conditions, but critics were swift in decrying the ruling. "Minority voters in places with a record of discrimination are now at greater risk of being disenfranchised than they have been in decades," said Jon Greenbaum of the Lawyers' Committee for Civil Rights Under Law.[6] After the decision, voter ID laws that had been previously blocked went into effect in several states.

In states where photo identification laws are in place, the closures or limited hours of state drivers' license offices can make it harder to get the needed ID. For example, Alabama came under fire in 2015 for closing down or reducing service at over 30 license offices after passing voter ID laws. Critics said the actions were discriminatory, as the office locations were in rural and majority-black counties. This would make it more difficult for lower-income and African American voters to obtain IDs. After public outcry, the governor partially reversed the decision.

Researchers are continuing to study the effects of voter ID laws on turnout and election results. A 2017 study published in the *Journal of Politics* concluded that strict photo ID laws decreased the turnout of minority voters in primaries and general elections, concluding that the laws "skew democracy in favor of whites and those on the political right."[5]

ELECTION RHETORIC

The 2016 presidential election was one of the most contentious in recent decades. Many polls predicted only a slim chance for Republican candidate Donald Trump to win over Democratic candidate Hillary Clinton. Trump's victory sparked renewed examinations of the roles of class, race, and other factors in US politics. Several of Trump's campaign promises centered on class and race. Trump promised to build a wall to crack down on illegal immigration from Mexico and vowed to impose tougher immigration standards. At one point, Trump promised to ban all Muslims from entering the United States. Sociologists in the *Harvard Business Review* found that Trump's speeches often focused on working-class values and what he saw as threats to the country. Perceived threats included immigrants, Muslims, and refugees.

Before, during, and after the election, a great deal of discussion surrounded white working-class voters in particular. Trump won a large share of voters who had not earned a college degree. Announcing that he was running for president, he remarked, "Sadly, the American dream is dead."[7] His campaign slogan was Make America Great Again. These statements seemed to resonate with white working-class voters, many of whom reportedly felt forgotten by politicians, mocked by perceived liberal elites, and excluded from economic progress. In recent decades, mortality rates among white people without college

Trump's "Make America Great Again" slogan was emblazoned on hats that he wore and sold during the campaign.

degrees had risen sharply from suicides, alcohol, and drugs. Lower-class white individuals were also experiencing increasing unemployment and declining wages.

Researchers suggest that some voters may also continue to feel threatened by a changing social and cultural landscape. They may not feel they have seen progress in the past decades, whereas other, non-white groups have. Some researchers criticize Democrats and other politicians for ignoring the working class and focusing on more affluent voters. They point out that members of the white underclass in poor areas have been experiencing real despair and downward mobility for years but have not had their voices heard.

American culture continues debating what it means to be white and working class. In 2016, J. D. Vance's book *Hillbilly Elegy: A Memoir of a Family and Culture in Crisis* became a best seller. Many critics hailed the account of Vance's family struggles as an important perspective into white working-class life. Some called it essential reading for understanding Trump's victory. However, many others took issue with the book's representations of the working class. In an editorial published in the *Washington Post*, attorney Betsy Rader, who was also born into poverty, wrote, "[The book's stereotypes] feed into the mythology that the undeserving poor make bad choices and are to blame for their own poverty, so taxpayer money should not be wasted on programs to help lift people out of poverty."[8]

DISCUSSION STARTERS

- Do you think people's race or class could affect their participation in politics? Is it important for everyone to be involved in politics? Why or why not?

- Did you follow any of the news surrounding the 2016 presidential election? How do you think issues of race and class factored into the presidential campaigns?

NINE

DIVIDED OR
UNITED?

Black Lives Matter began as a social media movement in 2013. The previous year, a Florida man named George Zimmerman killed African American teenager Trayvon Martin. Zimmerman's acquittal prompted activists Alicia Garza, Patrisse Cullors, and Opal Tometi to create the hashtag #BlackLivesMatter to draw attention to racial disparities in police violence and the value of African American lives. The online campaign soon evolved into a full-fledged movement. The group gained national attention with its demonstrations in Ferguson after Michael Brown's shooting.

The group's disruptive demonstrations, such as blocking freeways, have drawn critics, even among those who support the

At Black Lives Matter demonstrations around the country, activists have delivered messages that intersect with issues of class.

BLACK LIVES MATTER AND CLASS

"Black Lives Matter . . . is as much an example of a US-based class struggle as Occupy Wall Street was. To focus on the black poor is not to ignore others who also endure economic inequality. . . . In other words, any serious analysis of racial capitalism must recognize that to seek liberation for black people is also to destabilize inequality in the United States at large, and to create new possibilities for all who live here."[3]
—Barbara Ransby of *Dissent* magazine

group's mission. Others point out that protest must challenge what is accepted as normal. "Whether it's segregated lunch counters or voting rights or whether it's police violence—that's what protest does, and it challenges with varying degrees of intensity the status quo," remarked one individual who had been involved with the civil rights movement of the 1960s.[1]

Although the Black Lives Matter mission is based on racial justice, the formation and future of the movement has important intersections with economic justice. "The class divide is, in my opinion, one of the most important and overlooked factors in the rise of Black Lives Matter, led by a generation of college graduates and students," writes scholar Henry Louis Gates Jr. "I hear about it from my students at Harvard, about the pressure they feel to rise, yes, but also the necessity to then look back to lift others."[2]

HATRED DESCENDS ON CHARLOTTESVILLE

In August 2017, a rally of far-right extremists turned deadly. On August 11, hundreds of white nationalists, white supremacists, neo-Nazis, and Ku Klux Klan members descended on the University of Virginia in Charlottesville, Virginia. They gathered for a rally they called Unite the Right. Many identified themselves as part of the newly branded "alt-right" (short for "alternative right") movement, which is based around the idea of white nationalism. Carrying torches through the street, they evoked historical imagery of the Ku Klux Klan, although many wore polo shirts and khakis rather than white hoods. The next day, a rally participant drove his car into a crowd, injuring 19 and killing counterprotester Heather Heyer.

The violent clash in Charlottesville drew attention to the issues of class and race.

CHECKING PRIVILEGE

The idea of privilege often arises in conversations about class and race. Privilege is the concept that people of a certain group receive special unearned perks or advantages. Class privilege refers to advantages that someone of middle- or upper-class status might enjoy. White privilege refers to advantages that someone with white skin experiences that a person of color does not. Privilege can refer to things that a member of a group takes for granted and doesn't need to worry about on a daily basis. For example, white privilege could be the experience of white people seeing their own race widely represented on television, or the experience of a white teen shopping without being suspected of planning to shoplift.

Racist and anti-racist protesters faced off against each other in Charlottesville in 2017.

Those participating in nationalist rallies expressed resentment about the perceived plight of poor white Americans. Observers pointed out that well-educated, upper-middle-class white citizens have historically been involved in the United States' white supremacist movements, including those who founded the Ku Klux Klan. "Contrary to popular belief, white supremacy has not gestated on the fringes of American politics," wrote Christopher Petrella in the *Washington Post*. "Rather, it has flourished as a social movement grounded in respectability politics and led by elites."[4] According to Petrella, acknowledging this history is fundamental to overcoming white supremacy.

RACE AND PUBLIC IDENTITY

Some researchers criticize US society's focus on poverty and crime in minority populations while ignoring minorities who are part of the upper and middle class. Being a person of color in the upper classes can come with unique challenges and pressures. In her book *Blue-Chip Black*, Karyn R. Lacy describes how middle-class African Americans work to separate themselves from negative stereotypes and assumptions. They may dress differently so they will not be suspected of shoplifting. They may share their credentials to highlight their authority at work. Or they may feel the need to prove to people of the white middle class that they belong and are similar to them. Lacy points out that these acts of establishing public identity can be tiring.

BRINGING IT TOGETHER

In looking to make success in the United States an equal opportunity for all, some leaders are working to physically bring people together. Integration of

neighborhoods and communities will play a key role in closing equality gaps and uniting people of different backgrounds. Advocates call for grassroots efforts of community coalitions to build relationships and overcome segregation. Working together, the coalitions can brainstorm and strategize on plans such as new zoning policies and affordable housing.

From Flint to Ferguson and in every city in the United States, race and class are shaping the lives and interactions of Americans each day. They are also shaping continuing systems of inequality and the resulting calls for reform and justice. While people search

In protests against the government in 2017, people explicitly linked issues of racism and poverty.

for causes and solutions to divisive issues, questions on the roles of class and race will continue to arise. Is race or class more important than the other? Is it helpful to look at the effects of one over the other? Should they be addressed together?

Although the factors of race and class in the United States each have unique history, different types of impacts, and their own special challenges, they are deeply connected. It is likely that the two may never be fully untangled. Throughout the nation's history, the United States has had policies that intentionally or unintentionally reinforced divisions between different classes and races. As Americans face new challenges, class and race will continue to shape conversations around housing, education, employment, crime, environment, immigration, politics, and activism.

DISCUSSION STARTERS

- Why might it be important to think about class and race when debating current controversial topics?

- What is one surprising thing that you learned in this book? What do you still have questions about?

ESSENTIAL FACTS

SIGNIFICANT EVENTS

- The US government isolated and displaced Native Americans and also forced them to assimilate to white culture. Many Native Americans continue to live on reservations today.

- The end of the Civil War brought about an end to slavery but was followed by Jim Crow laws that continued to oppress African Americans in the South.

- Under President Franklin D. Roosevelt's New Deal, the US government created new housing agencies and policies. Many benefits did not apply to minorities. Practices such as redlining served to limit opportunities for African Americans and increase segregation.

- The civil rights movement of the 1960s paved the way for new social programs and reforms.

- The 2014 water crisis in Flint, Michigan, stirred up controversy because of officials' lack of response to help residents of the largely low-income and minority population.

- The 2014 police shooting of Michael Brown in Ferguson, Missouri, prompted protests and debates over race, class, and policing.

KEY PLAYERS

- US presidents including John F. Kennedy and Lyndon B. Johnson enacted social programs that sought to help close divisions of class and race.

- Immigrants to the United States, coming in search of better lives, have helped to shape the country's changing demographics.

- Black Lives Matter is an activist group that addresses racial justice along with economic justice.

IMPACT ON SOCIETY

The categories of class and race have deep connections to gaps in educational achievement, employment, and poverty. Ties between class and race can be traced back to programs and policies that often put people of color and low-income individuals at a disadvantage. The significance of class and race continues to be debated in areas such as housing, politics, immigration, and policing in the United States. Conversations about race and class also have an important role as people turn to protests and activism, such as in the Occupy Wall Street or Black Lives Matter movements.

QUOTE

"Negroes are not the only poor in the nation. There are nearly twice as many white poor as Negro, and therefore the struggle against poverty is not involved solely with color or racial discrimination but with elementary economic justice."

—*Martin Luther King Jr.*

GLOSSARY

ACQUITTAL
The act of setting free by declaring not guilty.

ASSIMILATE
The process of adopting the ways of another culture.

BIAS
Prejudice in favor of or against one thing, person, or group compared with another, usually in a way considered to be unfair.

CONSERVATIVE
Believing in small government and established social, economic, and political traditions and practices.

CORROSIVE
Causing damage through chemical reaction.

DE FACTO
Something that exists not by law but by social systems.

DE JURE
Something that exists by law.

DISENFRANCHISE
To deprive a group of a legal right.

EQUITY
The difference between a home's current market value and the remaining mortgage payments.

FORECLOSURE
The action of taking possession of a mortgaged property after the person who borrowed money can no longer make mortgage payments.

LIBERAL
Believing in large government and supporting new ideas and ways of behaving.

OPIOID
A class of drugs that act on the central nervous system to relieve pain.

SEGREGATE
To separate groups of people based on race, gender, ethnicity, or other factors.

SUBSIDIZE
To pay part of the cost of something in order to lower the price for the purchaser.

SUPREMACIST
Someone who believes people of a particular race, religion, or other category are better than other people.

TENANT
A person who owns or rents land or property.

ADDITIONAL
RESOURCES

SELECTED BIBLIOGRAPHY

Iceland, John, and Rima Wilkes. "Does Socioeconomic Status Matter?" *Social Problems* 53.2 (2006): 249. Web.

Katz-Fishman, Walda, and Jerome Scott. "Diversity and Equality: Race and Class in America." *Sociological Forum* 4.9 (1994): 569–81. Web.

O'Flaherty, Brendan. *The Economics of Race in the United States*. Cambridge, MA: Harvard, 2015. Print.

FURTHER READINGS

Eboch, M. M. *Race and Economics*. Minneapolis: Abdo, 2018.

Edwards, Sue Bradford. *What Are Race and Racism?* Minneapolis: Abdo, 2018.

Edwards, Sue Bradford, and Duchess Harris. *Black Lives Matter*. Minneapolis: Abdo, 2016.

ONLINE RESOURCES

To learn more about class and race, visit **abdobooklinks.com**. These links are routinely monitored and updated to provide the most current information available.

MORE INFORMATION

For more information on this subject, contact or visit the following organizations:

SMITHSONIAN NATIONAL MUSEUM OF AFRICAN AMERICAN HISTORY AND CULTURE
1400 Constitution Ave. NW
Washington, DC 20560
1-844-750-3012
nmaahc.si.edu

This museum documents African American life, history, and culture through exhibits and historical artifacts.

TENEMENT MUSEUM
103 Orchard Street
New York, NY 10002
1-877-975-3786
tenement.org

This interactive museum tells the stories of working-class immigrants in Manhattan, offering tours of recreated apartments as well as walking tours of the neighborhood. The museum also helps provide deeper understanding of today's immigration debates.

US DEPARTMENT OF HOUSING AND URBAN DEVELOPMENT (HUD)
451 Seventh Street SW
Washington, DC 20410
1-202-708-1112
hud.gov

HUD has many programs with the mission of providing affordable and nondiscriminatory housing.

SOURCE NOTES

CHAPTER 1. FIGHTING FOR FLINT

1. "Read the Letter from 'Little Miss Flint' That Stirred Obama to Visit Flint." *Los Angeles Times*. Los Angeles Times, 4 May 2016. Web. 16 Feb. 2018.

2. Reilly Morse. "Environmental Justice through the Eye of Hurricane Katrina." *Joint Center for Political and Economic Studies Institute*. Stanford University, 2008. Web. 16 Feb. 2018.

3. Marc Lamont Hill. *Nobody: Casualties of America's War on the Vulnerable, from Ferguson to Flint and Beyond*. New York: Atria, 2016. Print. 162.

4. Oona Goodin-Smith. "Flint Lead Pipe Replacement Program to Switch Hands in 2018." *M Live*. M Live, 1 Dec. 2017. Web. 16 Feb. 2018.

5. Julia Lurie. "Meet the Mom Who Helped Expose Flint's Toxic Water Nightmare." *Mother Jones*. Mother Jones, 21 Jan. 2016. Web. 7 Oct. 2017.

6. Trymaine Lee. "The Rust Belt: Once Mighty Cities in Decline." *MSNBC*. MSNBC, n.d. Web. 16 Feb. 2018.

7. Kristen Jordan Shamus. "How Race, Class Set the Stage for Flint Water Crisis." *Detroit Free Press*. Detroit Free Press, 23 Mar. 2016. Web. 1 Oct. 2017.

8. "The Flint Water Crisis: Systemic Racism through the Lens of Flint." *Michigan Civil Rights Commission*. State of Michigan, 17 Feb. 2017. Web. 16 Feb. 2018.

9. Brenden O'Flaherty. *The Economics of Race*. Cambridge, MA: Harvard, 2015. Print. 23.

CHAPTER 2. THIS LAND IS OUR LAND

1. Roger L. Nichols. *American Indians in US History*. Norman, OK: U of Oklahoma P, 2014. Print. 79.

2. "The Trail of Tears." *PBS*. PBS, n.d. Web. 16 Feb. 2018.

3. "Cleveland Signs Devastating Dawes Act into Law." *This Day in History*. History Channel, n.d. Web. 16 Feb. 2018.

4. "Frequently Asked Questions." *Bureau of Indian Affairs*. US Department of the Interior, n.d. Web. 16 Feb. 2018.

5. "American Indian Boarding Schools Haunt Many." *NPR*. NPR, 12 May 2008. Web. 16 Feb. 2018.

6. "Frequently Asked Questions."

7. Katherine Peralta. "Native Americans Left Behind in the Economic Recovery." *US News and World Report*. US News and World Report, 27 Nov. 2014. Web. 16 Feb. 2018.

8. Peralta, "Native Americans Left Behind in the Economic Recovery."

9. Peralta, "Native Americans Left Behind in the Economic Recovery."

10. "Who Is Indian, and What Makes a Person an Indian?" *National Museum of the American Indian*. Smithsonian, 26 Jan. 2011. Web. 16 Feb. 2018.

11. Tara Houska. "Houska: The Indian Problem Is Getting Worse—Isn't It Great?" *Indian Country Today*. Indian Country Today, 23 Sept. 2015. Web. 16 Feb. 2018.

CHAPTER 3. SLAVERY TO CITIZENSHIP

1. Walda Katz-Fishman and Jerome Scott. "Diversity and Equality: Race and Class in America." *Sociological Forum* 9.4 (1994): 573. Web.

2. Christopher Petrella. "Well-Educated Elites Are No Strangers to White Supremacy." *Washington Post*. Washington Post, 14 Aug. 2017. Web. 16 Feb. 2018.

3. Petrella, "Well-Educated Elites Are No Strangers to White Supremacy."

4. Lisa Ko. "Unwanted Sterilization and Eugenics Programs in the United States." *PBS*. PBS, 29 Jan. 2016. Web. 21 Oct. 2017.

5. "African Americans in WWII." *National Museum of the Pacific War*. National Museum of the Pacific War, n.d. Web. 29 Oct. 2017.

6. "Class in America: Identities Blue as Economy Changes." *NBC News*. NBC, 18 Mar. 2015. Web. 6 Oct. 2017.

CHAPTER 4. ALL IN THE NEIGHBORHOOD

1. Elizabeth Winkler. "'Snob Zoning' Is Racial Housing Segregation by Another Name." *Wonkblog*. Washington Post, 25 Sept. 2017. Web. 22 Oct. 2017.

2. Kendra Yoshinaga. "Race, School Ratings and Real Estate: A 'Legal Gray Area.'" *NPR Ed*. NPR, 10 Oct. 2016. Web. 16 Feb. 2018.

3. Terry Gross. "A 'Forgotten History' of How the US Government Segregated America." *NPR*. NPR, 3 May 2017. Web. 16 Feb. 2018.

4. Gross, "A 'Forgotten History' of How the US Government Segregated America."

5. Matt Wray and Annalee Newitz, eds. *White Trash: Race and Class in America*. New York: Routledge, 1997. Print. 18.

6. Katie Nodjimbadem. "The Racial Segregation of American Cities Was Anything but Accidental." *Smithsonian*. Smithsonian, 30 May 2017. Web. 30 Oct. 2017.

CHAPTER 5. THE CHANGING FACE OF AMERICA

1. "Modern Immigration Wave Brings 59 Million to US, Driving Population Growth and Change Through 2065." *Pew Research Center*. Pew, 28 Sept. 2015. Web. 11 Oct. 2017.

2. Anthony Daniel Perez and Charles Hirschman. "The Changing Racial and Ethnic Composition of the US Population: Emerging American Identities." *Population Development Review* 35.1 (2009): 1–51. Web.

3. Oksana Yakushko. "Immigration and Social Class." *The Oxford Handbook of Social Class in Counseling*. Oxford, 28 Mar. 2013. Web. 22 Oct. 2017.

4. Muzaffar Chishti, Faye Hipsman, and Isabel Ball. "Fifty Years On, the 1965 Immigration and Nationality Act Continues to Reshape the United States." *Migration Policy Institute*. Migration Policy Institute, 15 Oct. 2015. Web. 11 Nov. 2017.

5. Chishti, Hipsman, and Ball, "Fifty Years On."

6. "The Legacy of the 1965 Immigration Act." *Center for Immigration Studies*. CIS, 1 Sept. 1995. Web. 8 Nov. 2017.

7. "Modern Immigration Wave Brings 59 Million to US."

8. Michael Harriot. "When the Irish Weren't White." *The Root*. The Root, 17 Mar. 2017. Web. 16 Feb. 2018.

9. "Refugee Admissions." *US Department of State*. US Government, n.d. Web. 16 Feb. 2018.

10. Laura Koran. "Trump Administration Dramatically Scales Back Refugee Admissions." *CNN*. CNN, 27 Sept. 2017. Web. 4 Nov. 2017.

11. Jens Manuel Krogstad, Jeffrey S. Passel, and D'Vera Cohn. "5 Facts about Illegal Immigration in the US." *Pew Research Center*. Pew, 27 Apr. 2017. Web. 4 Nov. 2017.

12. Gustavo Solis. "How Undocumented Workers Pay Taxes, Buy Houses, and Open Businesses." *Desert Sun*. Desert Sun, 1 Dec. 2016. Web. 5 Nov. 2017.

13. Kevin R. Johnson. "The Intersection of Race and Class in US Immigration Law and Enforcement." *Duke Law*. Duke, 2009. Web. 8 Nov. 2017.

14. Johnson, "The Intersection of Race and Class in US Immigration Law and Enforcement."

15. William H. Frey. "Diversity Defines the Millennial Generation." *Brookings Institution*. Brookings Institution, 28 June 2016. Web. 11 Nov. 2017.

16. Gustavo López and Jens Manuel Krogstad. "Key Facts about Unauthorized Immigrants Enrolled in DACA." *Pew Research Center*. Pew, 25 Sept. 2017. Web. 16 Feb. 2018.

17. Catalina Amuedo-Dorantes and Francisco Antman. "Can Authorization Reduce Poverty among Undocumented Immigrants?" *Economic Letters* 147 (2016): 1–4. Web.

18. "Donald Trump Is Right: Congress Should Pass DACA." *Economist*. Economist, 9 Sept. 2017. Web. 11 Nov. 2017.

SOURCE NOTES
CONTINUED

CHAPTER 6. CLOSING THE GAPS

1. "20 Facts about US Inequality That Everyone Should Know." *Stanford Center for Poverty and Inequality*. Stanford, 2011. Web. 1 Oct. 2017.

2. "20 Facts about US Inequality That Everyone Should Know."

3. Jon Valant and Daniel A. Newark. "The Politics of Achievement Gaps." *Educational Researcher* 45.6 (2016): 332. Web.

4. Victoria Rideout and Vikki S. Katz. "Opportunity for All?" *Joan Ganz Cooney Center at Sesame Workshop*. Joan Ganz Cooney Center at Sesame Workshop, 2016. Web. 12 Nov. 2017.

5. Peter Dreier. "Black Lives Matter Joins a Long Line of Protest Movements That Have Shifted Public Opinion." *Salon*. Salon, 15 Aug. 2015. Web. 10 Nov. 2017.

6. Annie Lowrey. "The Economics of Occupy Wall Street." *Slate*. Slate, 5 Oct. 2011. Web. 16 Feb. 2018.

7. Sweta Vohra and Jordan Flaherty. "Race, Gender, and Occupy." *Occupy*. Occupy, 4 Apr. 2012. Web. 12 Nov. 2017.

8. Jamie Price. "Empowerment and the War on Poverty." *Sargent Shriver Peace Institute*. Sargent Shriver Peace Institute, 7 Jan. 2017. Web. 15 Dec. 2017.

9. Marianne Bertrand and Sendhil Mullainathan. "Are Emily and Greg More Employable than Lakisha and Jamal? A Field Experiment on Labor Market Discrimination." *American Economic Review* 94.4 (2004): 991. Web.

10. "Executive Order 10925." *Equal Employment Opportunity Commission*. EEOC, n.d. Web. 12 Nov. 2017.

CHAPTER 7. LAW ENFORCEMENT

1. "Chants." *Ferguson Response Network*. Ferguson Response Network, n.d. Web. 16 Feb. 2018.

2. Joe Soss and Vesla Weaver. "Police Are Our Government: Politics, Political Science, and the Policing of Race-Class Subjugated Communities." *Annual Review of Political Science* 20 (2017): 565–591. Web.

3. Soss and Weaver, "Police Are Our Government."

4. Damon Linkler. "Do American Cops Have a Race Problem? Or a Class Problem?" *Week*. Week, 5 Aug. 2015. Web. 5 Oct. 2017.

5. "Lyndon B. Johnson." *UC Santa Barbara*. US Santa Barbara, n.d. Web. 13 Nov. 2017.

6. Kareem Abdul-Jabbar. "The Coming Race War Won't Be about Race." *Time*. Time, 17 Aug. 2014. Web. 1 Oct. 2017.

7. Roy Walmsley. "World Prison Population List." *International Centre for Prison Studies*. ICPS, n.d. Web. 16 Feb. 2018.

8. John M. Eason. "Why Prison Building Will Continue Booming in Rural America." *The Conversation*. The Conversation, 12 Mar. 2017. Web. 16 Feb. 2018.

9. Elizabeth Hinton. "Why We Should Reconsider the War on Crime." *Time*. Time, 20 Mar. 2015. Web. 13 Nov. 2017.

10. Soss and Weaver, "Police Are Our Government."

11. Richard Nixon. "Remarks about an Intensified Program for Drug Abuse Prevention and Control." *American Presidency Project*. UC Santa Barbara, n.d. Web. 16 Feb. 2018.

12. Julie Netherland and Helena Hansen. "White Opioids: Pharmaceutical Race and the War on Drugs That Wasn't." *BioSocieties* 12.2 (2017): 217–38. Web.

13. Ojmarrh Mitchell and Michael S. Caudy. "Race Differences in Drug Offending and Drug Distribution Arrests." *Crime & Delinquency* 63.2 (2015): 91–112. Web.

14. "The DEA Years." *Drug Enforcement Administration*. Drug Enforcement Administration, n.d. Web. 16 Feb. 2018.

15. Kevin McKenzie. "Opioid Crisis Points to Racial Divide." *USA Today*. USA Today, 27 Mar. 2017. Web. 8 Nov. 2017.

16. Julie Hirschfeld Davis. "Trump Declares Opioid Crisis a 'Health Emergency' but Requests No Funds." *New York Times*. New York Times, 26 Oct. 2017. Web. 16 Feb. 2018.

17. McKenzie, "Opioid Crisis Points to Racial Divide."

CHAPTER 8. POLITICS AND POWER

1. "The Parties on the Eve of the 2016 Election." *Pew Research Center*. Pew, 13 Sept. 2016. Web. 16 Feb. 2018.

2. "Full Text of 'The Kerner Report Revisited.'" *Archive.org*. Internet Archive, n.d. Web. 9 Nov. 2017.

3. "February 29, 1968: Kerner Commission Reports on US Racial Inequality." *Learning Network*. New York Times, 29 Feb. 2012. Web. 16 Feb. 2018.

4. Daniel Laurison. "Social Class and Political Engagement in the United States." *Sociology Compass* 10.8 (2016): 684–97. Web.

5. Christopher Ingraham. "New Evidence That Voter ID Laws 'Skew Democracy' in Favor of White Republicans." *Washington Post*. Washington Post, 4 Feb. 2016. Web. 9 Mar. 2018.

6. Richard Wolf and Brad Heath. "Supreme Court Rules on Voting Rights: Now What?" *USA Today*. USA Today, 25 June 2013. Web. 9 Mar. 2018.

7. "Here's Donald Trump's Presidential Announcement Speech." *Time*. Time, 16 June 2015. Web. 16 Feb. 2018.

8. Betsy Rader. "I Was Born in Poverty in Appalachia. 'Hillbilly Elegy' Doesn't Speak for Me." *Washington Post*. Washington Post, 1 Sept. 2017. Web. 16 Feb. 2018.

CHAPTER 9. DIVIDED OR UNITED?

1. Elahe Izadi. "Black Lives Matter and America's Long History of Resisting Civil Rights Protesters." *Washington Post*. Washington Post, 19 Apr. 2016. Web. 16 Feb. 2018.

2. Henry Louis Gates Jr. "Black America and the Class Divide." *New York Times*. New York Times, 1 Feb. 2016. Web. 30 Sept. 2017.

3. Barbara Ransby. "The Class Politics of Black Lives Matter." *Dissent*. Dissent, 2015. Web. 16 Feb. 2018.

4. Christopher Petrella. "Well-Educated Elites Are No Strangers to White Supremacy." *Washington Post*. Washington Post, 14 Aug. 2017. Web. 16 Feb. 2018.

INDEX

ABOUT THE
AUTHORS

DUCHESS HARRIS, JD, PHD

Professor Harris is the chair of the American Studies department at Macalester College and curator of the Duchess Harris Collection of ABDO books. She is the author and coauthor of recently released ABDO books including *Hidden Human Computers: The Black Women of NASA*, *Black Lives Matter*, and *Race and Policing*.

Before working with ABDO, she authored several other books on the topics of race, culture, and American history. She served as an associate editor for *Litigation News*, the American Bar Association Section of Litigation's quarterly flagship publication, and was the first editor in chief of *Law Raza*, an interactive online journal covering race and the law, published at William Mitchell College of Law. She has earned a PhD in American Studies from the University of Minnesota and a JD from William Mitchell College of Law.

LAURA K. MURRAY

Laura K. Murray has written more than 50 nonfiction books for children. She lives in Minnesota.